"Congratulations, Dr. Johnson (Darrell), on a wonderful book depicting how dedication and determination can lead to wonderful goal accomplishments. Your special reference to "Foot Soldiers" brought a smile to my face. The book highlights how every experience in life and every person you meet and interact with is important. All of the experiences we encounter are paramount in our overall quest to do the best we can to educate young people to the highest degree possible. You have captured that passion in your first book. I know this will be a helpful, insightful guide to many education leaders! Well Done, My Friend!"

--Gloria J. Davis
Retired School Superintendent, Illinois and Kansas
Consultant
Regional Search Associate

"The words in this book are just as vivid and powerful as if they were being delivered in person by Dr. Darrell Johnson himself. He has given us this powerful, encouraging and inspiring memoir to affirm that through perseverance, determination, and commitment, one can succeed. Thank you, Dr. Johnson for sharing and caring through this literary volume."

-Dot Guthrie
Gaston County Board of Education
Gastonia, NC

"It is my very strong belief that if you work with children in any capacity, you should read this book. The wisdom of Dr. Darrell Johnson is clear, but heartfelt, as he "tells it like it is" as only he can. Having been raised by his grandmama in the projects, his perspective is both unique and sincere. He has truly become a "hedge" for all children, as his grandmama was a hedge for him. Dr. Johnson cared enough to spend his life teaching children they can achieve, "And Then Some." He spent his life teaching them they can break the cycle, "And Then Some." He spent his life teaching them that the sky is "not" the limit. They can go beyond! I am using his words because they are wise. His words of wisdom have helped me for many years, and now they can help you. Read his story! Continue his dream!"

-Fred Logan
Principal of Cleveland Academy of Leadership
Spartanburg, SC

"Dr. Johnson has shared life experiences that model what can be accomplished when we take full advantage of opportunities provided to us. This book will cause us to reflect on what we must do to address the educational needs of all children, and serves as a superb guide for developing leaders of tomorrow."

-Dr. Randy Bridges
Former Superintendent
Virginia, North Carolina and South Carolina

It Ain't In The Book

It Ain't In The Book

Dr. Darrell Johnson

Cover Design by Robert Grant

Published by

HadassahsCrownPublishing.com

Library of Congress Control Number: 2019940078

ISBN 978-0-9980269-9-2

Printed in the United States of America

This book is dedicated to the memory of Bennie Dexter Bennett: friend, brother, superintendent, and world changer who believed...And Then Some!

Contents

FOREWORD

Becoming a superintendent is life-changing. After accepting an offer to lead a South Carolina school district a few years ago, I met a veteran superintendent with a longer than average tenure. Introduced to him by a mutual colleague, I walked away feeling I had someone who not only understood the complexities of the job, but also had experience navigating those waters. Dr. Darrell Johnson has been a substitute teacher, recreational department gym leader, custodian, news reporter, teacher, assistant principal, principal, assistant superintendent and one of the nation's longest lasting superintendents. A ten-year consecutive span of being a superintendent qualifies him to write this book or any book, but it is the manner in which he simplifies the complexity of the systemic educational issues we face that propels us to pay close attention to his experiences and words.

As a full-time educational consultant for many years, I often wondered what those in the trenches thought after hearing an inspirational speech that drew standing ovations. Once back on the front lines of reality, those inspiring words quickly disappeared and educators had to face the harsh reality that the students we are called to educate today are different from any generation before them. Moreover, it requires a different vision and approach to be able to capture, inspire and teach them. Enter the arena with a leader like Darrell Johnson and your chances of winning grow. Dr. Johnson has a unique ability to tell it like it is, while developing positive relationships with others that create the right conditions for students to be successful. Great leaders don't create followers; they develop more leaders. Dr. Johnson has been developing leaders for many years and as you read through the pages that follow, you will gain a better understanding of the arduous tasks before today's leaders and teachers. Further, this book will help you draw deeper conclusions. The demands of leaders, while commonplace, are laborious. Failure has become normalized and an accepted practice. When the traumas of the world lay our children down in our classrooms, we need leaders like Darrell Johnson. Every school district/school deserves a great leader, not by chance, but by design. We know results cannot exceed the quality of its leaders and teachers. Dr. Johnson is a change maker with a track record of success everywhere he has entered the arena. *It Ain't In The Book* is engaging, relevant, poignant, inspiring and powerful. Every page is full of Dr. Johnson's insightful wisdom and his experience leading from the front reigns. Each chapter captures and inspires the reader to want more and you get it throughout this empowering version of what we all wish was taught in undergrad or graduate study. An appropriate title for a relevant time that calls for truth; a revelation that many of us don't know what we don't know. Darrell teaches us all to remain ready and willing to learn and grow while realizing, the most important lessons "ain't in the book."

Stephen G. Peters, Ed. D.
Superintendent of Laurens School District 55
Laurens, SC

When a person is able to look back on their life's work and see that they have held fast to their faith and lived honorably with family and friends, then they have a story to tell that we all would do well to listen to. And, oh my, does this book have stories! Every page speaks of the humanity and responsibility of family, leadership, friendship, living and learning. The stories are told with respectful humor and outright clarity. They make you think, feel, hope and be simply glad you picked up this book.

It Ain't In The Book has as its foundation the story of "being shaped by a praying grandmama" and it just grows from there. Over and over we are given a front row seat to practical wisdom that came from making sense of things that you just couldn't predict would happen.

It is a blessing to complete a satisfying career and to have learned so much from the unexpected and unpredictable experiences that came along on the journey. And it is wonderful to know that so many of the things that could prepare us for our journey, but were not in the book before are now in THIS book.

Dr. Lora Hodges
Center for Responsive Schools Executive Director

INTRODUCTION

For more than two decades, I thought about writing a book. I primarily wanted to celebrate the answered prayers of my Mama, Rev. Everleen Johnson. Mama was actually my grandmama. She reared my cousins and me in the projects in the small town of Clover, SC. She taught me how to get things done. I learned intuitively, somehow, to do what she expected. Sometimes, she did not say a word. Her facial expressions signaled what she wanted done. I quickly learned how to do what was asked and avoided spankings.

I spent my entire childhood with Mama. Her faith in God was steadfast. She was a praying woman whose religious beliefs were manifested in her grandchildren. She taught us how to fast, pray and trust in the Lord. These spiritual practices, combined with her intercessions, formed a "hedge" around me that has guided, protected and sustained me through numerous trials and tribulations. I am often reminded of Mama when I hear certain gospel songs. The lyrics to "We've Come This Far by Faith," for example, resonate with my soul as I think of her. A popular refrain in the song, "leaning and trusting on the Lord," bring back precious memories of Mama.

As I grew up and ventured away from home, there were subtle reminders of what Mama taught me as a little boy. Some expectations never change, especially dressing appropriately for church.

On one Sunday morning when I returned home from college, I knew Mama expected me to attend church. It was only a three-minute walk. Since I had been away for a couple of months, I decided to dress comfortably, but inappropriately for church. I was decked out in my suit, but I chose not to completely button up my shirt. The two top buttons were not fastened. I thought it was a good idea to "show off" my chest. After all, I had left home.

Boy was I in for a shock. As I walked down the aisle and prepared to sit down, I looked at Mama. I gave her a big smile. She didn't smile. Her eyes spoke to me. She did not say a word but I understood what she was asking. I immediately left the church and ran home. I went into the house, found a necktie, and put it on. Oh yeah, I knew to button the shirt all the way to the top and hustled back to church.

Back down the aisle I strolled. Mama looked me up and down. She nodded in the affirmative. She smiled and began to sing her favorite song: "If I Could Not Say a Word, I Would Just Wave My Hand." I knew I answered correctly. Lessons can be taught in many ways. Even though I progressed to college, Mama reminded me, in her own way, that "It Ain't In The Book."

My career has been more than she dreamed. She dreamed of my becoming a teacher. I became a principal. She wanted me to graduate from college. I earned a doctoral degree. Mama wanted me to be a role model for others.

Along this journey, the "hedge" has protected me regardless of where I worked. I was a recreation department gym leader, heating and plumbing assistant, hospital nursing attendant, full-time school custodian, high school and college basketball official, substitute teacher, newspaper city government and business reporter, middle and high school teacher, elementary and high school assistant principal, elementary school principal, director of student services, assistant superintendent, educational consultant and motivational speaker. I also was a university adjunct professor. Whew! All of these experiences were preparing me, in some way, to serve as a school superintendent.

It was my time. I paid my dues.

Twenty years later, the book is a reality. The vignettes within these pages allow me to share true stories about my experiences. Some are surprising. A few make you shake your head. Others make you wonder.

As you read this book, place yourself in my shoes. Imagine how you would react. At the end of each chapter, a question is posed for you to further consider the dilemma, possibly have a discussion and apply your own knowledge and experience. In my youth, I couldn't use the internet or google to answer problems. As Mama taught me, I had to trust in God because "It Ain't In The Book."

Mama's Boys— Dr. Johnson and Marc Witherspoon

ONE

TELL THEM ABOUT YOUR GRANDMAMA

It seemed as though Bennie Bennett always knew what advice to give in order to help a young brother out of a tough situation. We had previously discussed our positions in the school system as assistant superintendents. I worked for the Rock Hill School District. Bennie worked in Clover. We both wanted to test the waters for the superintendency.

We often talked about what we would do if we were given an opportunity to lead a school district. We agreed that our previous experiences as teachers, coaches, assistant principals, building level principals and district administrators had prepared us for the job. All we needed was an opportunity and we could make the adjustment to lead a school district.

Bennie led our venture to become superintendents. His journey was smoother than mine. He was a finalist in his first pursuit, and he nearly landed the first job he applied for and made a great showing. On his second attempt, he interviewed for a position and was named a finalist again. This time he landed the job. Bennie was selected as Superintendent of Newberry County School District. I was so happy and proud of him and knew that he was the right person for the job. There was no doubt in my mind that if anyone could lead a school district, Bennie was the right person. He was a proud man, and he insisted that I become a superintendent, too.

My journey, on the other hand, was somewhat rocky in comparison to Bennie's. I completed my resume, filled out applications and applied for a couple of positions.

During the first interview, I was a little nervous but answered the questions with some precision. Some precision when interviewing for a superintendent's position is not good because a fairly precise interview is not good enough. I did not get the job.

The next interview, which occurred about a month after the first one, was a position that I felt in my heart I would attain. It was a very small district in South Carolina and I did my homework. I researched the district and knew about the academics, athletics, and a little about the area. I was on my way to the interview and felt quite confident prior to walking into the room with the school board members.

The interview progressed without issues and I felt I answered all the questions correctly. My grammar was intact, as my subjects and verbs agreed. I discussed student achievement as well as the budget in the school district. My research was thorough and I had answers for all of their questions. My previous experiences in education made me a prime candidate for the job. My "A-game" was on display and I took care of business!

But, I did not get the job!

In fact, I did not make it into the top three finalists for the position. I was quite dejected as I rode home with the news. I wasn't sure what I was going to do. I was about to yield to the thought that maybe the superintendency was not for me. I could return and work at the district office and maybe one day be an assistant in Bennie's district.

Suddenly, my phone rang and it was Bennie checking to see how I did on this interview. As I shared the interview process with him and explained my answers, he simply listened and did not say a word. When I finished talking, he was silent for about 15 seconds and then he told me: "D, we need to talk young brother. Come on by the house tomorrow and we will figure this thing out so that I can help you get a job as a superintendent, too."

Bennie's plan to talk to me was not something that I had not heard before. We had conversations prior to this and he usually was right on target with his plans. Therefore, talking to him was worth my time. After all, when he was the head varsity basketball coach and I was a basketball official, he used his persuasive conversations to help me see things in a different light. We talked about the wonderful attributes of coaching and molding young boys into successful young men. He got me fired up and I ended up agreeing to coach the junior high basketball team. He watched my team practice one day and told me that we needed to talk. I figured it would be another one of those conversations in which he gave me a little encouragement and showed me how I could improve. I was wrong. He told me I was much better at officiating basketball than I was at coaching. He told me to keep at it and the coaching would sink in, too.

Nevertheless, I was not prepared for the conversation we had on that Friday after I was unsuccessful in my second interview for superintendent. As I reflect on our conversation that night at his home, the scene and his voice are as plain to me today as they were 13 years ago. I'll never forget that we were watching his beloved Los Angeles Lakers Basketball Team. He was steadily coaching the team from his recliner. He was all into the game and telling players what to do, as though they could hear him. "Really Bennie," I thought, as he coached and applauded the team's effort.

At half time, he broke away from the game and shared life-changing information with me. He looked me directly in the eye and told me I would never get a job as a superintendent using my current approach. He told me when you go to interview for these jobs, school board members do not want to hear all of the jargon you are using. He said he knows I have an English degree and that I know my subject matter quite well. However, he exclaimed, school board members don't want to hear all of that stuff you are talking about. "Stop trying to be a doctor in those interviews. Tell them about your grandmama!"

I was somewhat perplexed by this statement that Bennie had just exhorted to me. He was serious. He did not blink. His eyes were wide open and he was pointing that finger at me and I knew he was on a roll. I just could not understand what he meant by encouraging me to tell school board members about my grandmama.

In my mind, I was thinking that the Board doesn't know my grandmama, nor was she familiar with them. She was a praying grandmama; how could talking about her help me land a job as a superintendent?

At this point, Bennie just looked at me and there was a moment of silence. He did not say a word. His eyes told the story. Next, he began to speak and his message was powerful. In fact, the words changed my outlook on the situation. He said "D, tell them about your grandmama. Let them know you are just a country boy from Clover who was raised in the projects. Talk nicely to them and let them know how you respect everybody regardless of where they come from. Tell them how your grandmama taught you to put God first in everything. They need to know they can talk to you and trust you because your heart is in the right place for children."

He then proceeded to ask some questions that made so much sense that I wondered why I hadn't thought of this myself. He continued, "When you talk to your grandmama, how do you talk to her? Don't you make sure your words are clear and easily understood? You make eye contact, don't you?" He continued, "When you talk to her, you make sure what you're saying is clear, precise, and is easily understood. You make eye contact, speak from the heart and connect with her, don't you?" His suggestion that I simply talk to school board members during the interview was phenomenal.

You will never believe what happened...

I took Bennie's advice and reentered the interview circuit. I applied for a superintendent's position in two different school districts. The interviews were two weeks apart. As I prepared for the interviews, I followed Bennie's advice and told the board members about my grandmama. What happened during the next two interviews was indescribable.

During both interviews (with thoughts of my grandmama), I immediately began to connect with the board members. As I spoke to them and responded to their questions, in the back of my mind was Bennie constantly coaching me, "Tell them about your grandmama." I was deliberate, patient and engaged with the board members. I was not nervous and only imagined that I was making sure I conveyed the message I wanted to share. I was sure to present myself as someone who was appealing and pleasant- the way my grandmama had reared me. I informed them of my Christianity and that God is first in my life.

Perhaps one of the best ways to determine whether Bennie's words of wisdom worked for me was evident in the result of these two interviews. Both interviews went eminently well. In both cases, I informed the board of trustees that I had been reared by my grandmama and that I truly valued education.

The interviews were so successful that I was named a finalist in two different school districts at the same time! Telling them about my grandmama paid major dividends, while simultaneously creating a dilemma for me (and Bennie). Now, I would have to move forward and see if I could secure my first job as a superintendent.

I never would have dreamed that Bennie's simple advice would propel me into the finalist position for a job leading a school district. Bennie's method worked! I was selected as Superintendent of Greenwood School District 50. Thank the Lord for my grandmama-- and big brother Bennie.

It Ain't In The Book...

The Late Bennie Bennett and Dr. Johnson

enjoying a game of golf.

For Discussion

What is your personal favorite story that allows you to connect with others?

_____

_____

_____

_____

_____

_____

_____

_____

_____

_____

_____

_____

_____

_____

_____

_____

_____

TWO

TEARDROPS

"Teardrops can be misinterpreted. They represent joy. They represent pain. Sometimes tears just can't be explained...."

As I prepared to leave Clover to become Superintendent of Greenwood School District 50, I tearfully reflected on everything my grandmama had told me. She prepared me for this moment. I knew what I had to do.

First, I met with my Uncle Frank McClure, a devout Christian and chairman of our church's deacon board. He prayed, read scriptures, retold stories of biblical leaders and elaborated on their trials and tribulations. He encouraged me to be guided by a passage from the Bible: Joshua 1: 7-8 -- "Only be strong and very courageous, that you may observe to do according to all the law which Moses My servant commanded you; do not turn from it to the right hand or to the left, that you may prosper wherever you go."

Uncle Frank was tranquil in explaining this verse and the surrounding information for this passage. He explained that throughout my life, God had prepared me to be a leader. He ensured that I understood the adage that you would be amazed at how much can be accomplished if nobody cared who received the credit for a job well done. Uncle Frank gave me several scriptures to grasp for guidance. He prayed for me again; we shed some tears and I felt more comfortable about my departure. At the following church service, our pastor prayed a special prayer over me and anointed my head with oil.

At last, I was ready to depart for Greenwood. As the tears rolled down my cheeks, I knew God had big plans for me. The best was yet to come.

Sure enough, the beginning was phenomenal. My first official meeting in Greenwood School District 50 was a surprise for some people. But for those who knew me, it gave me a little reminder of where I came from.

I met with all the district's custodians! This was a group I felt comfortable dialoguing with because it was during my service as a school custodian that I learned the most about school operations. These individuals work tirelessly for the entire school district, and I wanted to ensure them I was counting on them to help me.

The custodians were beyond bewildered when I showed up at their meeting. However, that didn't upset their optimism. We agreed to work as a team to improve the district.

As I conducted a sharing session with the custodians, I was overcome with emotion. I reflected on my time in Clover vacuuming and waxing floors throughout the school. Preparing the schools for students and staff was the most critical time. Throughout all my custodial work, I never dreamed I would one day be the leader of a school district. I just thought about a familiar phrase: God is good all the time; and all the time, God is good. This meeting empowered me. It was now time to meet with the other members of the district team.

Prior to my first board meeting, there were two memorable interactions. I met two Greenwood County leaders who truly cared about the community. I was blessed to meet them, as they became invaluable friends throughout my tenure as superintendent.

My first indelible meeting occurred as I arrived at the district office for the board meeting. There was a gentleman already parked as I drove up. He got out of his car and stood at the door. I had never seen him before, but I'll never forget him. As I parked and exited my vehicle, he greeted me with a smile and a firm handshake. He said "Hi, I believe you are the new superintendent. My name is Dan, and I'd like to welcome you to Greenwood." After the warm welcome we chatted for a few moments. He never shared his occupation. I thought he was a nice guy. He said he looked forward to working with me. As we entered the building, he gave me his business card and I immediately noted he was Dan Wideman, Sheriff of Greenwood County.

During my first board meeting, I was a little overwhelmed; my eyes were a little cloudy. Somehow, I finally settled in and spoke with the board members as their employee. I was so thankful that this group of leaders gave a novice superintendent an opportunity to join a prestigious district. I hoped I could measure up to their expectations and even exceed them!

The other encouraging moment was also with a county leader. This time, Mrs. Edith Childs, a member of the Greenwood County Council who proudly donned one of her famous, colorful hats, invited me to her annual Back-to-

School Bash. I've attended many similar events, but this one was unique.

The crowd was large and enthusiastic. Councilwoman Childs vividly explained the moment and introduced me as the new superintendent. There were a few cheers and I addressed the group of parents and children. As I spoke, I couldn't help but notice an elderly gentleman who was crying. I hoped my message was not so boring that it brought tears to his eyes. I was very concerned, so after my speech, I mustered up enough courage to ask him why he was weeping.

I conversed with him. He told me he was 80 years old and explained the reason for the tears. His answer startled me. He responded, "I've seen a lot in my day. I never thought I would see a Black man leading Greenwood Schools. God bless you and trust Him."

I was moved by his words. As I began to dry my tears, I could only thank God for this tremendous opportunity.

We all left that site, but the memory- and tears- linger forever. For times like these....the answers are not in the book!

Uncle Frank with Dr. Johnson at a

University of South Carolina Basketball Game

Dr. Johnson and Uncle Frank after church

For Discussion

Share a time when you were overwhelmed with emotion.

_____

_____

_____

_____

_____

_____

_____

_____

_____

_____

_____

_____

_____

_____

_____

_____

THREE

THE SAINTS

I never understood why I had to attend these night meetings with Grandmama, Reverend Everleen Davis Johnson. I called her Mama. After all, I was just a little boy and I was around all of these elderly women. It was a regular occurrence as every Wednesday night at 6 PM I attended a prayer meeting with Mama. Mama was rearing me, as well as three of my first cousins. I was the youngest of the grandchildren and the last child she reared. Some of my relatives claimed I received preferential treatment.

As members of Mars Tabernacle Fire Baptized Holiness Church, Mama, a very proud woman who believed in serving God, was always beautifully dressed with a matching hat for church service. Mama loved the Lord and made sure all her "children" attended church every Sunday. We attended religiously, despite one of us "claiming" to not feel well. Our attendance for Sunday School was mandatory.

In addition to attending Sunday services, Mama and her church friends, who we referred to as The Saints, met each Wednesday at the home of one of the church members. Mama was president of the circle and she (we) never missed a meeting. The Saints had an awesome time at these prayer meetings and strangely enough, so did I. I guess you could say I was the tag-along "little Saint."

Each week, the Saints sang songs, prayed and read the Bible. They focused on a specific chapter, intensely discussing the verses. On numerous occasions, they asked me to read some of the scriptures. I'm not sure if this was their way of keeping me from wandering throughout the house or if they liked the way I read. I also recited many scriptures because of "my practicing" at home with Mama. I obliged their requests and patiently read because, after all, these were our seniors. If I didn't read slowly and correctly, Sister Patterson, the elder member of the circle, asked me to repeat it. She either wanted me to slow down or she wanted to be sure I was learning, too. Sometimes I had to explain my interpretation of the scriptures, which probably prepared me for school or life.

At the end of each prayer meeting, Mama prayed. She was skilled in praying and often closed out the service with her, and my, favorite song: "If I Could Not Say a Word, I'd Just Wave My Hand."

By the way, another great ritual I especially enjoyed at these meetings was the home-cooked meals. All of the Saints doubled as marvelous chefs. My mouth waters every time I think about the crispy-fried chicken, fresh corn, tomatoes, collard greens, black-eyed peas and sweet potato custard. I can't leave out the delicious sweet tea. Yummy!

Talk about experiences that you don't understand. I thought about the similarities between Mama and me and wondered if these prayer meetings were preparing me for something greater in life. After all, I became an avid reader in Sunday School, recited scriptures to our congregation and later became Sunday School Superintendent. Was there a premonition here or just divine intervention? I wasn't sure because when it comes to occurrences like these... It Ain't In The Book.

Mama—Rev. Everleen Johnson

For Discussion

What early experiences shaped your character?

_____

_____

_____

_____

_____

_____

_____

_____

_____

_____

_____

_____

_____

_____

_____

_____

_____

_____

FOUR

30-THREE-30

As a leader in a school district, it is inevitable that numerous questions will be asked that must be answered. These questions, although they may seem minor to the leader, are very serious to the person who presents them. Every question deserves an answer-- verbal or non-verbal. Leaders often have problems when they fail to answer or when they don't expend the appropriate amount of time.

In leadership meetings with principals and directors, I encourage everyone to employ the 30-THREE-30 method whenever possible. Questions, whether posed by students, parents, business leaders, community residents, elected officials or others, can be handled in the timeframe of one of the following categories: 30 seconds, three minutes, or 30 minutes. While most requests can be answered within one of these categories, the leader must always be prepared to use the right time frame.

I recall a direct question that was posed to me during my first year as superintendent. It was not a difficult inquiry but one that had to be answered immediately. Choosing the right timeframe for the response was critical. Perhaps the main reason this inquiry still lingers in my spirit is because of the person who asked the question.

The day started as a routine morning. I was invited to attend a meeting for 30 specially-invited guests to hear the platform of a candidate running for the office of President of the United States of America. The presidential candidate's tone was relaxing. He was quite eloquent as he described his "hope" for a new America. He mesmerized the small audience and had everyone's undivided attention. At the conclusion of his speech, he met one-on-one with each attendee. His demeanor was very smooth as he candidly posed his question to me. His inquiry was very clear yet personal. His question, simply put, was "Dr. Johnson, if I am elected President of the United States of America, how could I assist you as Superintendent of Greenwood School District 50?"

At this point, I was a little startled but not nervous. I thought of my 30-THREE-30 method. Although I contemplated giving him a 30-minute answer, I knew three minutes was more than enough time to engage this candidate. Nevertheless, I concluded that a 30-second answer would suffice.

As a new superintendent, I knew I had to represent because my peers Bennie Bennett in Newberry, SC and Russell Booker in Spartanburg, SC would critique my response. With this thought in the back of my mind, I calmly answered his question, smiled and shook his hand as we took a photograph. I told him he had my support. I also encouraged him to stay calm (or something to that effect). A few weeks later, I watched him repeat my answer on live television!

Who would have guessed that I had answered a question from then Senator Barack Obama while he was campaigning in Greenwood, SC? On this particular night on television, Senator Obama was debating Senator John McCain. I was very proud as I watched Senator Obama swagger over toward Senator McCain. In response to a question about education, Senator Obama repeated the answer I had given him a few weeks earlier at the invitation-only meeting. Senator Obama's statement, and my answer, was simply "No more unfunded mandates for education." Wow! I was so proud of Senator Obama's recalling my answer (and probably someone else's too) that I can still hear him repeating the answer and utilizing my now famous 30-THREE-30 method. What a great answer. What a great debate….

On the other hand, there are times when 30-second answers will not suffice. This is especially true when talking to a parent -- who happens to be at work -- about her son who is in the third grade. Here's what happened during our THREE-minute phone conversation.

A teacher at an elementary school where I was principal had a problem dealing with a student repeatedly using profanity in class. The student kept using the word "hell." It frustrated the teacher and she asked for my assistance. I called the student to my office and explained to him that using the word "hell" was unacceptable. While the student was in my office, I decided to call his mother at work. I wanted to talk about him repeatedly saying "hell" in class. It was upsetting other students and disheartening the teacher. Once the receptionist connected my call to the mother, the first comment the mother made to me was "Ah, hell, what has he done now?" Although shocked at her response, I quickly realized where her son picked up the bad language. I immediately stated that her son had been sent to the office and I wanted permission to work with him on his vocabulary. She then said, "Hell, y'all always calling about something. You can work with him, though." I responded that I believe he is a good boy and can be an outstanding student. I just needed her permission to be his mentor. We talked about the importance of a good education and she was agreeable with my helping improve her child's vocabulary skills. Her next question shocked me. She said, "Are you sure you don't want me to come down to that school and talk with my son?"

My response, quite off the cuff, was direct. I told her, "Hell, naw. I don't need you to come to the school. I got this!"

Mom said, "Okay, have a good day and I'll talk to you later. Goodbye." She hung up, and I couldn't believe my response but I knew we had made a connection. It took the THREE-minute response but the change would impact a lifetime for her son, and me, too.

Although routinely mentioned, there are many times that the leader must be prepared to have a 30-minute conversation to share information or explain an idea or program. These meetings typically take place with large groups or influential members of the community.

Personally, I enjoyed these meetings because they allowed me to totally engage in a discussion that encourages participants to let their passion flow. They provided an opportunity to speak candidly about beliefs and knowledge on the topic.

One such topic for me occurred during a meeting with business and community leaders about higher education, focusing on affording every child an opportunity to pursue the next level of education. The key tenet, several of us believed, was money. Was it possible to set up a program where students could pursue their dream and money not be an obstacle? Could we navigate the old answer of "No, because" and move to a better scenario of "Yes, if?" The discussion was powerful! We talked about the pros and cons of higher education. Which is best for students in Greenwood: two-year college or four-year college? We debated whether this should be required of every student. I was so proud of the leadership team from Greenwood County! These leaders, men and women, were so professional discussing this topic. They were candid. They were forward thinkers. Most impressive, they displayed care and concern for all students in our county. They recognized now was the time to take a leap that would reap tremendous rewards for the future.

As a result of this and other 30-plus-minute meetings, an outstanding program was launched. In 2017, Greenwood County business and community leaders unveiled the Greenwood Promise, a $5 million public-partner venture aimed at providing scholarship funds to assist students residing in Greenwood County with tuition support to earn an associate's degree at Piedmont Technical College. Phase One of the Greenwood Promise pays tuition for students earning an associate's degree. The funding, referred to as "final dollars," is paid after a student has exhausted all other financial options in the form of grants and scholarships.

This was a bold move! Every time I think of how much this immediately helped students throughout the county, I realize how blessed I was as superintendent. Just think; we have awesome business and community leaders who sacrifice to serve as generous benefactors. This is unprecedented.

And...It Ain't In The Book.

44th President of the United States Barack Obama

with Dr. Johnson

For Discussion

How will you prepare ahead of time to respond to difficult

questions when you're put on the spot?

What legacy will you leave?

_____

_____

_____

_____

_____

_____

_____

_____

_____

_____

_____

_____

_____

_____

_____

FIVE

MARTIN LUTHER THE KING

It started out just like any other school day during the month of February. The weather was cool. The sun was shining brightly and I did not have a care in the world. For some reason, I wanted to go by and see how our kindergarten students were faring as they began their educational journey. I selected an elementary school and decided that this would be a great place to go in and observe. I arrived at the school, stopped by the office and headed immediately to a kindergarten classroom. Super excited for some reason, and really not knowing why, I entered the classroom quietly. I didn't want to interrupt the lesson. I should also note that as a school district, we were working on safety protocols. We wanted our kindergarten students to yell "stranger" if they saw someone they did not recognize.

After a brief observation of the classroom, I began

to walk around and watch students completing their work. The teacher decided to join me, as she asked students questions. As we walked around the class, one little boy was hyper focused on his lesson. He really didn't notice me. His hair was blonde and his eyes were bright blue. His pupils sparkled. His smile was precious. When he peered up from his paper, he smiled and kept on writing. However, at this point, the teacher interjected a question that I will never forget. She asked him, "Do you know who this gentleman is?" The little boy looked at her and smiled again. Next, he looked at me again with a grin on his face and kept on writing. He was definitely on task. I was inclined to believe he was telling himself that surely the teacher would not ask him to answer such a ridiculous question about the superintendent. Nevertheless, the teacher asked the question again. The young man looked up at her and gave her another smile. He then answered the question. He proudly told the teacher, "Everybody knows him!" I felt so great at this moment. I was thinking that even though I've only been in Greenwood for seven months, our kindergarten students recognize me. This superintendent gig is going to be great. I felt I had connected. My mission was being accomplished. Go Johnson, go. You are on it!

Not quite so fast with the personal accolades. The teacher did as we expect them to do. She probed further. Her next question tested the young boy's knowledge as well as my confidence. Her question now metamorphosed to, "If you know who he is, what is his name?" At this point, the little boy was visibly frustrated at the numerous interruptions and repeated questions about the gentleman who stood beside her. The little boy decided to respond his own way. He stopped writing, looked the teacher directly in the eye, and slammed his pencil down on his desk. He then exclaimed: "Everyone knows him! He is Martin Luther the King."

Totally bewildered by his response, I did what every first-year superintendent should do... I remained calm, smiled and walked away from the little boy. I left the classroom in total shock. Just when I thought I had arrived as a superintendent, a kindergartener reminded me of one very important fact of life: If you want to know where you truly stand in life, just ask a kindergartener.

It Ain't In The Book!

For Discussion

Are you visible and known?

Discuss the difference and the importance of each.

_____

_____

_____

_____

_____

_____

_____

_____

_____

_____

_____

_____

_____

_____

_____

_____

_____

_____

_____

SIX

BENNIE AND THE BOYZ

Parliament's Mothership Connection released a song entitled "Star Child" in 1975 that sums up what it was like to be new superintendents in 2006. The lyrics to the song resonated with me. They provided an answer, too. Note the following: "If you hear any noise it's just me and the boys. Hit me, you gotta hit the band." These words were perfect for what I was about to endure as a superintendent. The lyrics helped me realize that to make it along this journey, I needed some other members of the "band" to be successful. Fortunately for me, I connected with two of the most spectacular superintendents in South Carolina, Bennie Bennett in Newberry and Russell Booker in Spartanburg. Each one of us came from humble backgrounds. Bennie grew up in the small town of Gable, SC. There were dirt roads and he often spoke of "cropping tobacco." Russell was reared in the rural area of

Spartanburg, SC as a country boy. I, on the otherhand, grew up in the projects of Clover, SC, having spent a lot of time playing baseball in the street in front of our apartment. We knew how tough life could be without an education. Our unyielding faith in God and love for others was integral to our "team." We made sure we kept this idea in the forefront of our plans.

We all were about to learn how to lead school districts. Individually, we were alone on an island. Together, we immediately realized we could navigate this terrain. We accepted our positions within six months of each other. Bennie brought us all together and once he did, we were totally united, like blood brothers. Bennie was the oldest, I was the middle child and Russell was the little brother. At local and state meetings, if you saw one of us, you saw the other two. We established a close-knit bond based upon trust and love for each other.

As superintendents, we knew we had to have each other's back. We all knew each other's family quite well, including birthdays, graduations and important family events. We traveled together, listened to each other's speeches and school plans, and shared an award-winning tournament golf team. The three of us, as well as former

Orangeburg Superintendent Walt Tobin, were a formidable team. (The golf matches were quite interesting because while competing against other teams, we also had a little challenge going on among ourselves.) We were tight.

When it came time to conduct business in our districts, we were well aware of what each was facing. We talked about how to handle upset board members, unruly parents and residents who did not have children's best interests at heart. We all knew that as servant leaders, our priority was to ensure we gave our best effort every day. It was our responsibility to ensure that every child in our district had an equal opportunity to rise to the next level in education. Since we were all working in a position we never dreamed of, we made sure we never forgot where our own journeys began.

As a crew, the three of us had monthly meetings in which we had our own personal inbox exercises. Each of us brought three issues to discuss. Each shared his plans while the other two offered pros and cons on the situation. We also suggested how we might handle the situations if it were in our district. It was a true brotherhood. There were many times when we did not agree with another's handling of a particular matter. Yet, our closeness allowed us to share where we disagreed with the other's actions. No one's feelings were hurt. We had fun addressing issues, laughing and supporting each other.

Often, Bennie, Russell and I met early in the morning in Columbia and had breakfast prior to our statewide superintendent meetings. At this gathering, we reminded each other to remain optimistic. It was important to stay calm and make sure that if we made a statement, we thought before we spoke. We also agreed that if we felt strongly about issues, we made our concerns known in a constructive manner.

This friendship between the three of us lasted for 12 years. It ended abruptly when Bennie was killed in an automobile accident on a Saturday afternoon. The fatal accident occurred a few hours after we were together playing golf. This was one of the saddest days of my life. It hurts every time I think of the last days the three of us spent together.

We had traveled to Atlanta for a charitable golf event that raised college funds for underprivileged students. After checking in to our hotel, we talked with unfamiliar basketball players from across the United States in the hotel lobby on Friday afternoon. Nevertheless,

Bennie, whose passion as an outstanding basketball coach is known throughout the southeast, talked to them about winning the game of life. He had their undivided attention. A few moments later, Bennie spoke with Russell's youngest son by phone about how to improve his jump shot. Next, we talked to Bennie's daughter and he reminded her that his "brothers" (Russell, Charles Joseph and I) would always be there for her. Bennie was Charles' former basketball coach and they attended the same church. That night, we all enjoyed Bennie's favorite dish, a bone-in steak. Dinner was fantastic, and we unknowingly shared one of our last special times together as a team.

On Saturday, we participated in the golf outing. Our routines were in order but on this occasion, Bennie was our captain for the entire match. We usually rotated the captain duties but this time, for some reason, Bennie was captain all day. He was in total control, just like a big brother. On the last hole we played, number 18, we had a long, 60-foot birdie putt. Bennie instructed Russell, Charles and me to get in the golf cart because he was going to make the putt. Immediately, we began walking. As I looked over my shoulder, Bennie putted the ball down the hill and it landed dead center in the middle of the cup. "Birdie, my brothers!"

Bennie exclaimed as he walked to the golf cart to receive his well-deserved high fives. Bam! He did it again.

We departed for home from Atlanta that Saturday afternoon. After returning to South Carolina, Bennie stopped by his office in Newberry. He had a meeting that night. Russell, Charles and I continued to our homes. As I walked in my door, my phone rang. I was informed that Bennie had been killed in an automobile accident a few minutes prior to my receiving the phone call.

The news was devastating and totally threw me for a loop. I called Russell. He was shocked. We both cried about the loss of our dear brother. Russell then reminded me of the last text that Bennie sent us. It read, "Friends!!!!!!!"

Losing Bennie was huge for us. We lost a brother.... someone we looked up to for so many things. It is unexplainable.

It Ain't In The Book.

Bennie Bennett, Dr. Russell Booker and Dr. Johnson

At Urban League Banquet Honoring Dr. Booker

Charles Joseph, Bennie Bennett and

Dr. Johnson at a golf tournament

For Discussion

Who do you look up to? Who is your mentor?

Who do you depend on during tough times?

_____

_____

_____

_____

_____

_____

_____

_____

_____

_____

_____

_____

_____

_____

_____

_____

_____

SEVEN

TEACHERS

Teachers are phenomenal! They are the bread and butter of any school system. These professionals have the power to make or break a system. Fortunately for me, Greenwood 50 had teachers who truly cared about our students. Many teachers came early, stayed late and taught with smiles on their faces.

Personally, I realized the blessing in working with these instructional leaders who don't teach a subject matter- they teach students. I wholeheartedly believe that the most important place in a school is the classroom. When the door is shut, the relationship between the teacher and student is of utmost importance. This relationship far outweighs the contacts students may have with the principal. They see other administrators and district office staff in the building. But every day, every class period, students interact with the teacher. This interaction is pivotal because our system must be about teaching and learning.

I was very proud of the energetic teachers in Greenwood School District 50. I made it a point to leave the office and visit the classrooms on a regular basis, although I didn't evaluate teachers. I only observed and took pictures of teachers and students interacting. I "tweeted" pictures from observations, and visiting the classrooms was the highlight of many of my days. Many times, and probably somewhat surprisingly, our teachers allowed me to do a mini-lesson (in English/Language Arts classes). When time permitted, and somehow it always did, teachers were gracious enough to allow me to quiz students about their learning. The students impressed me with their ability to expound on their subject matter. The teachers smiled and students gave each other high fives. Some students, I surmise, looked at me and wondered who is this guy and why is he here? After I had been in the district for a few years, the teachers got used to my visits. We became comfortable with each other. Often when asking questions of students, I'd promise pizza for the class if someone answered correctly! (Principals were aware because they provided the pizza. I know, smart plan!) I had two favorite questions. They both were easy. The first was, "Spell your name correctly." It sounded easy, but it wasn't. Remember, I used to teach English. The second question also caused great thought and eventual research. The question was, "What is a diacritic dot?" This puzzled many students. I offered a clue. Think about a "tittle." You guessed it; students immediately utilized their Chromebooks and spent more time on the Google site. I thoroughly enjoyed it when I returned and they couldn't wait to share the answer. The return visit, they later learned, did not involve a pizza. Such joy this brought to my soul. The students were doing what we expected, learning.

There were so many outstanding happenings in my 13 years in Greenwood that I can't list them all. However, a few events that come to mind are the class visits into the band and chorus rooms at Greenwood High School. I'll never forget the day our chorus director allowed me to "direct" the outstanding Greenwood Show Choir. They sang magnificently despite my directing. I also vividly recall a high school math class at Greenwood High School. Every time I visited this class, my schedule was thrown totally out of kilter. This was because of the authentic engagement the math teacher had with her students. All eyes were on the teacher and the dialogue was genuine; I often became engaged in their discussions. I was usually delayed for other appointments. I later talked to several students in that class who told me they enjoyed the class. It was their favorite because the teacher taught the subject matter and lessons about life. Even when this teacher had adversity in her own family, she still put her students first. She challenged them daily.

Equally impressive were teachers at Emerald High School. They had some phenomenal project-based learning events. These included the "Hooverville" Great Depression, Stop Hunger Now and the Coffee House focusing on Free Trade. My conversations and participation at these events were delightful. Perhaps one of my favorite moments at Emerald High School was the Socratic Seminar on the Harlem Renaissance. The teachers invited me to participate, and I gladly accepted. I was eager to join in this debate with students because this was a topic that I enjoyed. The teachers and students were surprised with my knowledge of the writers during this period in history. They later found out that I wrote my master's thesis on *God's Trombones*. It was a major part of the Harlem Renaissance.

On the day of the Socratic Seminar, I battled toe-to-toe with the students. They were well-prepared and excellent at debating. (Many of them had participated on debate teams at the middle school.) We both had our facts together. It was intense. They were sharp and made some great points that I had not thought about 30 years ago. If a neutral judge had scored the debate, the winner would have been the students. I accepted the defeat gracefully because the teachers were teaching and students were learning. I win every time. You gotta love it....

It Ain't In The Book.

For Discussion

Who are the true heroes? How do you recognize them?

_____

_____

_____

_____

_____

_____

_____

_____

_____

_____

_____

_____

_____

_____

_____

_____

_____

EIGHT

WHERE IS YOUR HELICOPTER?

Learning to read is one of the most exciting times in a student's life. It is a time that is transformational and momentous, and it must be celebrated.

As superintendent, there is an inspiring story about Rosa who was extra excited about learning how to read. One of our literacy coaches at an elementary school shared her excitement about Rosa with me. Rosa, who was from a home in which there was very little support for reading, was inspired after the literacy coach worked diligently to prepare her to become an avid reader.

I eagerly accepted an invitation to meet Rosa. I'll never forget the Monday morning trip to the elementary school. I saw the literacy coach standing in the foyer of the building. The literary coach had this gigantic smile on her face. She walked briskly over to me and excitedly exclaimed, "Dr. Johnson, I have some awesome news for you. I have been working closely with the student and she has improved her reading score by nearly 40 points! She adores reading and now that she has learned how to read, she enjoys reading to everybody. In fact, we told her about you and she wanted to read a story to you."

After hearing this excitement from the literacy coach, I told her that I wanted to experience this little girl's love for reading. This request from the teacher caused me to immediately flashback to the day when I was interviewing for the job to become Superintendent of Greenwood District 50. On the meet-the-candidate night for the superintendent interviewees, we were in the Greenwood Federal Building. Teachers had opportunities to ask questions and to learn more information about the candidates before the selection of the next superintendent was made. I was bombarded with so many questions from the district literacy and language arts teachers that I was totally hyped about their curiosity. As a former English teacher, the questions they were asking were right up my alley and I had a feeling that at some point during my tenure, if I were to secure the job, there would be a time in which we could celebrate reading. Perhaps Rosa reading to me was going to be a defining moment in my career. I believed that the time had come for me to personally hear Rosa's excitement for reading. The anticipated joy, unfortunately, had to wait. Rosa was absent. I was sad because I was eager to witness this success story.

Later that week, the literacy coach emailed me a video of Rosa reading to me. I was still eager to hear her read. I immediately opened the email and began watching the video. Rosa wore her hair in small braids and had a marvelous smile. Excitement beamed from her brown eyes as she announced the name of her book *No David*. She energetically began to read the book to me as though I was actually there in person. The rhythm and pace of her reading were perfectly executed. She enunciated all the syllables in the words with precision. The book was interesting and engaging in all aspects. It was as though I was with the character in the book because Rosa was so eloquent in her reading to me. Then, it happened completely out of nowhere. I was not ready for the next few words Rosa stated. As she read the next sentence from *No David,* Rosa calmly paused her reading, raised her head up above the book and looked directly in the lens of the camera and asked me a direct question. She shouted, "Dr. Johnson, are you paying attention?" I immediately shook my head several times in the affirmative and exclaimed back to her, "Yes, I'm paying attention!" It seemed as though Rosa was sitting in front of me in person. It was a surreal moment that I'll always remember. Without skipping a beat, Rosa had already returned to reading the book and completed the story without any interruptions from me. At the completion of the book, Rosa smiled and the video ended. I was totally shocked after the video but elated this student was enjoying reading. This would not be my last encounter with Rosa....

The Lord works in mysterious ways and has a way to bring things full circle. About a month later, as fate would have it, our board of trustees was having a noon meeting at Rosa's school. As I was walking with Gerald Witt, an assistant superintendent, to the meeting room, students began exiting the cafeteria to return to class. I was observing the students when I noticed one student had gotten out of line, broke into a very fast run and headed my way. Before I could recognize what was happening, the student was airborne and landed in my arms.

The student, whose voice I recognized because I couldn't see her face, then asked, "Dr. Johnson, where is your helicopter?" It was Rosa.

I was totally caught off guard and had no clue what Rosa was asking. Nevertheless, Mr. Witt whispered in my ear that Rosa was probably referring to the mode of transportation that the president normally arrives in on trips. She was thinking that since the president travels around in a helicopter, surely as the leader of the school district I had arrived in a helicopter, too. Rosa wanted to see my helicopter. I told her that I came in a car. She just stared at me for a second, totally ignored my statement, took my hand, and told me to come on and let's go to the classroom. She then gasped, "I will read a book to you." She led our group down the hallway. We went into her class and she had already chosen a book. Her teacher informed me that she was so proud of her reading skills that she wanted to read books all the time. She had been reading books to other teachers, students, custodians, cafeteria workers, and anyone who took the time to listen to her read.

The joy and excitement of Rosa learning to read brought tears to my eyes. Her passion for reading made me recall that reading is not just fundamental. Reading is transformational! The lesson I learned from Rosa about reading was very simple. It does not matter whether you arrive in a helicopter, Volkswagen or a Ferrari, you still can listen and enjoy a first-grader reading.

It Ain't In The Book...

Kewan Witt admires Dr. Johnson's fresh haircut.

For Discussion

What do you celebrate?

What areas need more celebration?

_____

_____

_____

_____

_____

_____

_____

_____

_____

_____

_____

_____

_____

_____

_____

_____

_____

_____

·   **NINE**

BOARD CHAIRPERSONS

One of the most integral aspects of being a superintendent is working with the board of trustees. How one manages this relationship will determine how long one remains in the role of superintendent. A major key to longevity with the board of trustees is learning how to work cooperatively with the school board chairperson. Whether the chairperson is elected or appointed, this person is charged with not only representing other trustees but also the entire district -- students, teachers, parents, businesses and the community at large. Developing this relationship proved to be critical during my tenure as superintendent.

I knew going in that establishing trust with the board chair was a priority. I was well-versed in this from my doctoral dissertation research entitled *Superintendent's Perspective on Minority School Board Members*, that although the board's (including the chairperson's) primary function is formulating the policy and approving the budget, they must approve any recommendations made by the superintendent. Teamwork is a requirement. Working side-by-side with the board chairperson caused me to quickly learn to adjust my individual plans and work from a team concept and accept the ideas of external stakeholders.

Sometimes we disagreed, yet I kept my values. There was always diplomacy during our discussions and I'm thankful we always kept our focus on children. The conversations centered on teaching and learning. We knew that regardless of what actions we were attempting, we had to think about the impact on the classroom.

It is important to note that throughout this process, we maintained our statesmanship while keeping the strength to represent our positions. We exhibited sensitivity and had the flexibility to disagree without being disagreeable. We knew that we could not go along with plans just to get along. We kept it "real" with each other and found tactful ways to express our differing opinions. I guess one can recall in the story of the emperor having on no clothes that someone had to tell the emperor the truth. In my situation, there were times that I had to find a tactful way to make my point. Sometimes it worked; sometimes it didn't. Either way, I learned immensely from these interactions. The experiences, positive and negative, made me a well-rounded superintendent.

Perhaps my biggest challenge of working with the board chairman occurred during my first year. It happened during my first two weeks in the position. Imagine beginning the job on July 1. Excitement abounds and you look forward to learning about the district and its challenges. You map out a 90-day plan to look and learn. Then, something hits you out of nowhere. Bam! The board of trustees informs you, for the first time, that we must immediately initiate a building plan. This plan, which was never discussed during the interviews, is huge. It includes spending $150 million to build new schools and make facility improvements at others. I was totally startled and unsure of what to do. This would be my first venture as superintendent. I was prepped for curriculum and instruction. Building schools, a $150 million project right out of the gate, was mind boggling. Nevertheless, I did what I knew best. I prayed and decided to lean on my educational and life experiences. I focused on the building plan and worked closely with the board chairperson. After all, my doctoral research indicated this was the direction I should take. I heeded my own advice and off to work I went.

I knew that I could work with the board chairperson. I had not counted on working with more than one. As it turned out, these relationships proved critical in completing the building program.

In my thirteen years as Superintendent of Greenwood School District 50, I worked closely with three different school board chairpersons. Each chairperson was fully committed to improving our district, carrying out the district's mission and placing high value on students, teachers and support staff. Each wanted to ensure that a premium amount of attention was placed on teaching and learning. They insisted that every student would be afforded an opportunity to achieve a first-class, high-quality education that would prepare them for a four-year college, two-year technical education, military service or the workforce. The care and concern for the entire district exhibited by each chairperson was optimal. Their desire to put the district first by sacrificing their personal time truly impressed me.

Each chair, nevertheless, had an individual style of leadership. They were similar in many areas but of course there were differences, too. Each one's tenure was perfect for the time frame that the district was going through. Their leadership styles forced me to adapt my leadership skills to their method of governing from a board perspective.

My first board chair was an amazing leader. She was well-respected throughout the community and state. She also served a term as president of the state school board association. I was truly amazed with how graceful she was in the midst of difficulty. She was a visionary who was willing to take a strong stance on issues that she believed moved our district forward. She knew the district was in desperate need of facilities. Despite tremendous opposition from a small but vocal group in our community, she spearheaded the $150 million building campaign. Talk about strength and wisdom; she led this effort alongside an inexperienced, first-year superintendent, me. I constantly learned how to navigate the landscape in a positive manner. She was adept at explaining the big picture so that the plan was easily understood. Together we met with educators, business leaders, parents, and community groups to explain our rationale for building new schools. Although we had tremendous support, there were a few individuals who totally opposed the building program. This opposition did not deter her and she continued her plight with a smile on her face and only positive words for all groups. I was new on the job but had to learn quickly. To top it off, she kept us on target even though the nation's economy crumbled in 2009 just as we kicked off our program. Also during the recession, the district's budget was cut by $5 million, yet she didn't waiver in her philosophy and the district continued to prosper. In fact, we were also able to implement the first of what would be numerous choice and magnet programs. We started at the middle school level with an Arts Communication Theatre School (ACTS) and followed it with a Science Technology Engineering Math (STEM) School.

My second board chair was a powerful, well-respected business owner. Everyone knew how much she loved the school district as was evidenced by her serving numerous terms on the school board. As the chairperson, she was savvy and kept the building initiative as a primary focus. She supported other programs as well. She was a proud graduate of Greenwood High School and very much engaged with academic and athletic programs throughout the district. Since she was vice-chair during the initial $150 million building program, continuing this effort was second nature to her. I was particularly impressed with her steadfastness and allegiance to the program. She was very meticulous in keeping the building program transparent for the community. As a major supporter of teachers, she ensured they were a priority. She encouraged teachers and administrators to venture out and connect with other districts in our state and nation.

Perhaps most noticeable about her was her visibility in the community, especially at sporting events. She was a supportive member of the booster club and was industrious in her efforts working with them. When not working as a member of the booster club, she attended games and amidst other parents, cheering on our teams. Her ability to work with so many different groups and talk candidly with them about issues were innate. She was not one to mince words, and her strength was in directly answering questions and keeping a meeting progressing.

My third board chair was a combination of the first two leaders. As the former athletic director and head football coach of powerful state-championship teams in Greenwood, he was revered by everyone. His ability to adapt to various situations was impressive. I note that he too was a strong supporter of the building program and had to make some tough decisions as we continued to improve facilities. Although athletics is what he was known for in many areas, his passion for children and teacher recognition was superior. Under his leadership, we began a program entitled "Learning Over Lunch," in which board members attended a different school each month for lunch. During this time, teachers showcased lessons while students demonstrated their learning. This allowed board members to interact one-on-one with faculty and students on their turf in a non-threatening manner. This board chair also initiated a time during board meetings to showcase teachers and support staff members of the month.

Working alongside these three different board chairpersons, I observed how different chairpersons utilized their skills for the best interest of students and teachers. As superintendent, I listened, watched, learned...and then some!

It Ain't In The Book........................

Dr. Johnson and Board Chairperson Shell Dulla

TEN

BUILDING BLOCKS

Some days I laugh. Some days I sing. Some days I cry. Every day I pray! Leaders know that each day might bring joy or pain. Some days, it brings both. One thing for certain is adversity is omnipresent. It is ready to creep into an organization at any time. The key is being ready to confront the hindrance and keep moving forward.

Serving as a superintendent can be a challenging position. There is so much to learn prior to taking the job. There is much more to learn once you are on the job and beginning to make major decisions that impact people's lives. I often wonder why some of the situations I dealt with are not taught in college. There are numerous projects to complete and papers to write. The board and I discussed nearly every issue one could imagine. Nevertheless, we missed one. This issue had to be addressed during my first month on the job as superintendent. Here's how it all unfolded.

The first task assigned to me by our school board was to implement a $150 million building program. That's right, a $150 million facility plan right out of the gate! It was a big and bold move in 2006. At the time, the district was serving 10 percent of the population in more than 70 portable classrooms. The plan was to build several new schools and make improvements at the other facilities. We used an Installment Purchase Bond (IPB) Program. IPB allowed us to proceed and keep the tax rate at the same level for 25 years. We shared this plan with parents, business leaders and community residents. Everything was progressing, but as expected, there were some people who were adamantly opposed to the building program. The adversity came forward.

I'll never forget the message that was waiting on me one Friday afternoon during my second week on the job. A person, who was a candidate for a seat on the school board, left an envelope for me. The candidate followed up with a voice message letting me know of the personal delivery. My curiosity was quickly answered when I opened the envelope. It was a lawsuit opposing the building plan. The candidate didn't file the lawsuit but wanted me to know they supported the suit 110%.

I was totally shocked and baffled. How could anyone not support a facility program that would benefit all children? It would, in my opinion, benefit our entire community. At one elementary school, the entire third grade was housed in portable classrooms. Facilities were deteriorating at other locations and now was the time to implement the building program.

I was new, but I knew how to fight back. After all, I had a praying grandmama and had held numerous positions to prepare me for this moment. Despite the lawsuit, the board continued to implement the building program. The person who delivered the lawsuit to me was elected to the school board. This new member was adamant and regularly showed opposition to the building program, but the other board members stood firm. They agreed this was the best course of action and held fast to what they believed in. It was a tumultuous time during our board meetings. The board member attempted to sway others to vote against the program, but his attempts were in vain. They listened but didn't agree to scrap the program.

After several months of the new board member opposing the building plan, we were finally able to secure the financial paperwork. We broke ground on our first project. We were now building schools for the future. Whew! It happened so fast. As a first-year superintendent, I realized how important it was to keep our board members and the public informed of all activities involving the building program. We ensured transparency.

It was a tough road for a couple months but fortunately, we were successful. Now, 12 years after the fact, our facilities are astounding. We receive numerous compliments and parents and community leaders are proud. I often note that if we were not faithful to our mission to complete the program when we did, the economic crash in 2009 would have prevented us from moving forward.

Sometimes as a superintendent you must hold fast to your convictions and proceed with what you know is right for children. The obstacles are very heavy, but you must be in it to win it and do what's best for children. It was a shock that a person running for the board would take this position. In the end, standing firm for facilities for all children was the best thing to do...

It Ain't In The Book.

For Discussion

How do you interact with and respond to leadership?

What is important when building key relationships?

_____

_____

_____

_____

_____

_____

_____

_____

_____

_____

_____

_____

_____

_____

_____

_____

_____

ELEVEN

FOOT SOLDIERS

Every leader knows it is important to have people in their circle who have a good understanding of the community. These individuals may not work in the school system, but they deeply care for children and are vested in their community. I refer to them as "foot soldiers."

Foot soldiers have the innate ability to be proactive. They prepare the leader for what's happening in the community -- good and bad. This support group has its finger on the pulse. They have connections the leader may not have, and they usually are well-respected in their neighborhoods. Often, these individuals are not educators, yet they know about the educated workforce.

There were numerous groups of foot soldiers who helped me navigate the terrain in Greenwood for 13 years. Although I could spend a great deal of time describing each one, I will only focus on three. These three groups include the Wednesday morning Men's Prayer Group, the Golden Girls and Mentoring for Success.

The Men's Prayer Group is astounding! These men, led by Jim Furman, a local car dealer, and Dan Wideman, the sheriff whom I met on my first day in Greenwood, made me appreciate being a leader in Greenwood. Members included men from all walks of life. We called each other brother. There were car dealers, insurance agents, business owners, physicians, retirees, ministers, law enforcement officers, college educators, and general laborers. What I liked most about this group is everyone left their titles at the door.

We met at 7 AM and said a prayer before eating breakfast. After breakfast, the men rotated and shared biblical lessons that were applicable to our daily lives. Each brother had his own style and method for showing God's love. It was truly a brotherhood in which everyone cared about each other. It seems we had been lifelong friends because we connected so well. I was impressed with their willingness to take care of those in need in our community. They were especially supportive of our students. Each Christmas, we collected funds to help a needy family or two. One year our group collected enough money to provide

Christmas for an entire family of four. The men were proud to help and did not seek any recognition for this effort. It was just the work of the Lord.

The second group of foot soldiers is known in Greenwood as the "Golden Girls." These outstanding ladies, most of them grandmamas, caused me to reflect on my childhood. Here I go again; more than 45 years later, I am meeting with a group of senior ladies. Similar to the prayer meetings for my grandmama, these Golden Girls were praying for me. In fact, the Golden Girls had to come to my rescue at a time when my life demanded their support.

When I first arrived in Greenwood, there were controversies that needed to be addressed. A tense community meeting was held in which I was under attack as the new superintendent. A member of the Golden Girls attended the meeting and quickly connected with me. She informed me that just like my grandmama, this group would be there to support me. They attended board meetings and spoke up during necessary times in the community.

Perhaps the one moment that I will never forget occurred at a Golden Girls' meeting. One of the members told me that everything would be fine. She implored me to keep focused on the children in our district. She said I just needed a good meal prepared the way my grandmama used to do it. I agreed to attend and see if they could "burn in the kitchen" like the Saints did when I was a little boy.

The banquet night arrived. It was in the winter and I did not feel well at all on this night. I was very weak and did not have an appetite. I didn't feel like being around anyone, but I had given the Golden Girls my word that I would attend. At the banquet, one of the ladies noticed that I was under the weather. She told me not to worry and that she had a remedy that would make me feel better. I was a little worried about the remedy because my grandmama had quite a few. These remedies usually worked but the taste was not appealing. Did she plan to give me castor oil like we took when I lived in the projects? I was not sure that I could handle this, but I knew the Golden Girls had my best interest at heart. They had adopted me as one of their sons.

To my surprise, one member of their group was also under the weather, perhaps with the flu. Although I felt badly for her, I decided that if she was taking the remedy, so would I. The Golden Girls made a concoction for us to drink. They told me that if I drank this concoction, which had some type of charcoal in it from the GNC store, I would feel better in the morning. I truly did not want to drink it, but I couldn't feel worse. However, my trust in these ladies led me to drink it.

By the next morning, I felt 100% better and truly appreciated this concern from the Golden Girls. It was a miracle, and I am forever grateful to this group of ladies. I must also note that as a show of their appreciation and support for me, they gave me a Golden Girls' shirt that had a special inscription on it: "Supporter!"

The third group of foot soldiers is one that I never dreamed about. Upon my arrival in Greenwood, I noticed that the lowest performing subgroup on standardized tests in the district were African American males in our middle schools. It was obvious that this group of young men needed the most assistance.

Since there were very few African-American male teachers in the district, I issued a challenge for African-American males in the Greenwood community to join me in assisting these young men. I didn't think I'd receive an affirmative response and was preparing to reach out to the Men's Prayer Group and the Golden Girls.

Boy, oh boy, was I surprised!

At our first meeting, more than 30 African-American males showed up and were willing to work with me to mentor boys. We immediately started a Mentoring for Success Program. It was active for my entire 13 years as superintendent, led by State Senator Floyd Nicholson, the mayor at the time. He was very positive and he assured me that the mentors would show up and take care of business. He was right. The group was comprised of adult male African-American volunteer mentors who have a vested interest in the well-being of boys in our district. Members of the club included local industry and professional workers, retired educators, pastors, local and state-elected officials and District 50 employees. One goal of the program was to help bridge the gap in economic and social development for these middle school participants. The young men were recommended to the program by family and community members, teachers, counselors and ministers.

Mentoring for Success Program met with these boys on a regular basis. They encouraged and motivated students on how to be successful in school and in life. In addition to mentoring, the group has been actively participating in cultural experiences, both locally and regionally. The program accompanied the young men on cultural experiences to colleges and universities in the

Carolinas and Georgia. It also led visits to museums, businesses and historical sites.

Perhaps one of the most impressive aspects of the group was their dedication in not only time but also personal financial donations to fund the activities and events. Senator Nicholson, who was a former middle school administrator, took the lead again and established an annual golf tournament, "Tee Off for the Kids." This event coupled, with other donations from members and supporters, enabled the group to provide $1,000 scholarships to the young men upon graduation from either of our two high schools. To date, the program has provided $58,000 in scholarships for these young men.

Who would have thought that we could pull off this feat? It Ain't In The Book.

Mentoring for Success

For Discussion

How will you identify and engage your foot soldiers?

_____

_____

_____

_____

_____

_____

_____

_____

_____

_____

_____

_____

_____

_____

_____

_____

_____

_____

TWELVE

DID YOU HEAR THAT?

A good leader listens. He understands the value in allowing others to feel comfortable enough to say what is on their minds. Whether their thoughts are supportive or critical of the organization, the leader knows that everyone is entitled to his or her own opinion.

When I listen to other people making comments about my performance or the performance of our organization, my mind always reflects on what I learned in my conversation with my Uncle Frank. Prior to my arrival in Greenwood, Uncle Frank and I had some very candid discussions. He emphasized the importance of not only listening to people but also hearing what they say. Or, as he explained, what they were "trying to say." Paying attention to all the surrounding details, real and perceived, is important.

Uncle Frank was right. His words of wisdom have been employed numerous times during my 13-year tenure as superintendent. He sometimes challenged my listening ability as he shared various passages from Greek scholars. He later quizzed me on what they meant and whether I truly heard what they said. One stands out from the rest. It states, "The art of an educated mind is the ability to entertain an idea and not accept it." I must admit that when Uncle Frank shared this with me, I didn't see how it would come into play in my role. However, his words of advice have proven beneficial time and time again.

As leaders, we are often confronted with people who have different viewpoints. Nevertheless, we must always listen because sometimes other people have better ideas than we do. We must listen carefully so that what they say is what we hear. I recall a couple of occasions in which I may have heard something different from what was said. In the first example, I had to listen closely to realize that I missed the first message. For some reason, I didn't hear what the people said.

It is important for leaders to have an outlet to perform well in their career. Leadership jobs can be stressful if the leader does not have an outlet. My outlet was officiating college basketball. I was a member of the Atlantic Coast Conference, Mid-Eastern Athletic Conference, Big South Conference, Central Collegiate Athletic Conference and a few others. Running up and down the court was great exercise. It gave me time to stay involved in an activity I enjoyed, officiating.

I recall one night when I was officiating a NCAA Division I college basketball game. It was not just a regular season game nor a conference tournament. This game was occurring during the NCAA Division I Basketball Tournament. That's right, March Madness! What I recall about the game may surprise some people. I flew in for the game at Purdue University and it snowed. My hype for the game didn't allow the snow to faze me. Notre Dame was one of the participating teams. I surmise there were about 10,000 fans at the game on this night. They were yelling and screaming loudly as I ran down the basketball court. I made a call and felt good. As I was running down the court, I heard fans yelling in unison "You, You!" after I made a call. I felt appreciated because these good people recognized an educator, a superintendent, who was having a good, tournament game.

As we, officials and players, walked to the free-throw line, I listened to the chant of the crowd again. This time I realized what I heard was not what they were saying. I thought the fans were saying "You, You!" when they were saying, "Boo, Boo!" Boy, did I feel some kind of way! I thought of Uncle Frank's message. "You gotta listen to truly hear what they are saying."

In the other scenario, I was listening (carefully) and therefore able to actively hear what was said. The listening occurred during a board meeting. It was a heated discussion and a board member didn't feel that people were listening to the point he was attempting to make. The day after the meeting, he came to my office for our heart-to-heart conversation. We were discussing some items that he wanted the board to consider. He talked at length about what he wanted the district to accomplish and how he wanted it done. I told him, quite candidly, that when he speaks at board meetings we all listen to what he says. However, I also told the board member that his passion is so great that others, including me, sometimes miss his message. The board member looked at me and nodded in the affirmative. He explained what he wanted to accomplish and shared the plan with me. He recognized that I was not only listening to his words, but I was hearing the message.

At our subsequent board meetings, he began to share ideas in a totally different manner. The other board members, and I, listened to a totally different message and heard it in a totally different way...

It Ain't In The Book....

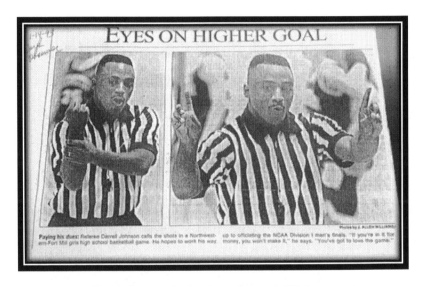

Dr. Johnson is featured as a NCAA

Division I College Basketball Official.

THIRTEEN

I KNEW IT

I knew it was time to leave Greenwood School District 50 during the annual Mentoring for Success Celebration Banquet on May 16, 2018. On this warm night, we were preparing to recognize nine members of our Being on Winning Teams in Education (BOWTIE) Club in the Genesis Education Center Board Room. We've had this celebration at least ten times. On this night, my spirit was at ease. I was impressed with how impeccably dressed our young men were for this occasion. They looked debonair, decked out in nice dress shirts, as well as bright and colorful bowties. Each of the boys had grown into young men and were preparing for high school graduation in the coming weeks.

That night, as usual, the adult members of our Mentoring for Success Program were clad in their suits and bowties as well. It was amazing witnessing the dedication of these adult mentors. They answered my challenge 13 years ago and, on this night, they were still involved. As I recalled the $41,000 in scholarships we awarded the boys over the years, my heart filled with joy. I was blessed to work with these men who knew that our future begins with our youth. To top it off, Senator Floyd Nicholson, who spearheaded this mentor effort, was present to support these young men. God is good.

The BOWTIE Club Members from Greenwood and Emerald High Schools were assembled, along with their families. As one young man spoke of his initial experience as a student in Greenwood School District 50, which happened to be my first year as superintendent, I listened intently and reflected on those first weeks.

As I looked at him and recalled his primary years, I noticed his mother smiling proudly. She then made eye contact with me, smiled and nodded her head in the affirmative. Her hair, which had been silky and shiny black twelve years ago, had now turned gray. My hair twelve years ago was black with waves. I had a part on the left side, and I thought I was cool. This night, I recognized my hair had disappeared, and my head was bald. I recalled conversations with this mother and an All-Star Award she gave me at a pivotal time during my first year. It was comforting then and I relived that presentation for a few moments.

As I continued to reflect, my eyes clouded and I was unable to control my emotions. These first graders had grown up to be fine young men. They were about to graduate in two weeks. At this moment I could seemingly hear my grandmama's voice. She was saying, "Darrell, you did good. I'm proud of you." I knew it was time to depart because I had done my best, and it was time to move on so that the next superintendent could continue the journey and take the school district to a higher level...

It Ain't In The Book...it's in your heart!

Mentee Tatravion Burton, Emerald High School's

Superintendent for a Day, with Dr. Johnson

Mentoring for Success with Dr. Johnson

at a Charlotte Hornet's Game

For Discussion

Do you know when to walk away?

_____

_____

_____

_____

_____

_____

_____

_____

_____

_____

_____

_____

_____

_____

_____

FOURTEEN

RANNIE

Mary Johnson, affectionately known as "Rannie" to her grandchildren and "MJ" to others, was my mother. Although quite petite in stature, she was a beautiful and very strong-willed lady. (In fact, my mother was a model, too. She was fine!)

MJ obtained her beautician's license from a university in New York City and worked in that field for ten years. She later worked 31 years at Nabisco Company, where she was known to be charming yet serious about her profession. Her work ethic was instilled in my siblings, Sherri and Lance, and me. MJ told us to always get the job done without making excuses. Whether I was a school custodian, teacher, principal or even a superintendent, her advice was the same -- take care of business and move forward.

Although diagnosed with stage-four cancer, MJ fought it valiantly for seven years and without a complaint. I recall dealing with a difficult situation in Greenwood School District 50 during her final days. I believed she could provide me guidance on how to resolve the matter. I was with MJ and although she was not feeling well, she knew I was struggling to solve an issue. Her words were soft and pleasant. She said, "Do your job and all will be fine. That's what Mama would expect you to do. Go get it done and you'll be fine. I guarantee it."

She sat on her bed and looked me in the eyes and smiled for a few moments. MJ used this final moment in her life to help and inspire me at the same time. She told me that throughout my life, I had been prepared from a little boy to handle these situations. She reminded me of the lessons learned while tagging along with my grandmama, reading scriptures in Sunday School, respecting all people regardless of who they were or where they came from and acknowledging that everyone should be loved. She told me, in essence, that the best way to solve that particular problem is to pray and ask God for guidance and put my trust in him. Your faith in God, she noted, will see you through! After all, as she helped me realize, the answer to many problems ain't in the book.

And now, as I write this chapter about her, she calmly listens in her bed during these final moments of life. As I read the aforementioned parts of this chapter, my mother is listening intently and looking at me with a bright smile on her face. My sister Sherri, a nurse, also listens as I read this passage to MJ. She is about to transition but is holding on until Lance arrives. I finish reading and Lance enters. MJ smiles as he talks to her and Sherri pays close attention to her vital signs. We are all there by her side as she transitions out of this world. MJ closes her eyes, as we acknowledge that Rannie has transitioned. It's difficult to explain, but this is definitely not in the book. It's in her spirit. She will always be with us- and then some!

Mary Johnson, Mother of Dr. Johnson

For Discussion

What personal challenges have you faced? How did you

balance those while remaining loyal to your career?

_____

_____

_____

_____

_____

_____

_____

_____

_____

_____

_____

_____

_____

_____

_____

ACKNOWLEDGEMENTS

God is Good!

First, I give thanks to my Lord and Savior for blessing me and ordering my steps in His word. I have been writing this book for a long time. My inspirations for this book are my grandmama, mother and son.

I had a praying grandmama, Reverend Everleen Johnson, who made it a priority for her entire family to trust and believe in God. A special honor goes to her because even though her education was limited, she found joy in motivating her grandchildren to excel to their highest aptitude. She always made sure I completed my school work and respected my teachers. "Mama," as we referred to her, expected my relatives and me to put God first in everything we did. There were many discussions held with her that I did not understand at the time. However, over the years, I saw clearly how Mama prepared me for life.

After more than 30 years as an educator, I realize

that memorizing Bible scriptures at home, participating in Sunday School and paying attention to the preacher's sermons were invaluable. These lessons equipped me for numerous challenges. I learned early to trust God, put Him first and fear nothing. This faith has enabled me to have numerous accomplishments in life. In all, I give God the glory because I am truly blessed. In fact, I believe the Lord has shown me favor because of the sacrifices of my grandmama. As they used to say when I was a little boy, "I'm reaping the benefits of a lot of prayer." I pray other grandmamas will keep the faith in their grandsons. The young boys may not appear to be listening, but, trust me, they are paying attention. Someday, I believe, other boys being reared by their grandmamas will also achieve the success and make their grandmamas proud, too.

Perhaps my deepest gratitude is reserved for my mother, Mary Frances Johnson. I called her "MJ." She was a trooper who did not take no for an answer, nor did she accept excuses. MJ's vision, inspiration and guidance were critical to my success as a leader. Regardless of how tough a situation appeared, her belief in me was unfailing. "Remember what Mama taught you? That's what I expect from you, and nothing less." I will always recall her beautiful smile. Her voice was soft but stern. Her eyes, I note, always seemed to have a message for me. "You can do it, Darrell. We know you can. You have been blessed."

I always think of my deceased son, Darnell. We lost him as a baby, and I often wonder what it would have been like to have my son tagging along beside me. It's a tough thought, but I try to talk to other boys the way I would have talked to him. Often, I look at his sister, Keyurshia, and just imagine. She's the apple of my eye and I pray that she, too, will continue with God's favor.

I also want to thank my family members who pushed me. Their belief in me when sometimes I wondered about myself was inspiring. Their encouragement was ever-present. They took as much joy in my accomplishments as I did. Sometimes they were more excited than me. I love them!

Two educators, Bennie Bennett and Russell Booker, were like brothers to me. We enjoyed learning to be superintendents together. Neither of us knew what to do for sure when we first started. But, we all trusted God and knew how to pray. We were best friends. We laughed. We argued. We cried. After all, we were brothers.

Thank you to Dr. Stephen Peters, Dr. Lora Hodges,

Dr. Randy Bridges, Gloria J. Davis, Fred Logan, Robert Grant, Dr. Shelia Counts and Jonathan Graves for their contributions to the book. I appreciate Hadassah's Crown Publishing, LLC for patiently and professionally leading the publishing path.

A special thanks goes to my Greenwood School District 50 Family! These guys are the greatest. It was indeed a pleasure to work with all of you. I am so grateful for the district office staff. Even though I was "new" and had no family in the area, you accepted me and laughed at some of my jokes. I am especially impressed at how professional you were while being friendly at the same time. We celebrated birthdays and mourned our losses. Most of all, we were family.

The community leaders, parents, church members, board members and others are too numerous to name. This was a fabulous group who provided enormous support for 13 years. I'll never forget the uplifting revivals or the prayers that were sent up for me.

What I will recall is when all is said and done about my tenure in Greenwood, SC.....

It Ain't In The Book!

ABOUT THE AUTHOR

Innovative. Progressive. Passionate.

These three words capture the essence of an educational leader who believes in children. Dr. Darrell Johnson served 13 years as superintendent of Greenwood School District 50 in Greenwood, SC. The son of Mary Johnson was born in Washington, D.C. and reared by his grandmama in the small town of Clover, SC. For more than 30 years, Dr. Johnson has pursued his passion of making a difference in the lives of children. While obtaining his teaching credentials in the mid-1980s, he worked as a school custodian and substitute teacher. After teaching language arts at the secondary level, Dr. Johnson served as an elementary school principal, then as an assistant superintendent before becoming a superintendent. In 2004, he earned his doctorate in education from South Carolina State University. During this time, he still found time to officiate NCAA Division I college basketball games for more than twenty-five years.

The accomplishments of Dr. Johnson include

completing $200 million in building facilities and implementing 12 magnet and choice programs. In 2017, his district kicked off the Greenwood Promise, a $5 million public-partner venture aimed at providing scholarship money to assist students who are Greenwood County residents with tuition support to earn an associate's degree. What stands out most about Dr. Johnson is his energy, indefatigability and dedication to the children, families and wider community he serves. He is passionate about creating the conditions for every child to develop the necessary core academic and social-emotional competencies for success at school and for their futures. He is also an active, engaged member of his community, volunteering and serving on local community foundation boards. Dr. Johnson also provides insights into school leadership, human development and essentials for our children to become fully engaged, productive citizens of the world. His question for leaders is simple. "If the game is on the line for children, do you want the ball?" As leaders, Dr. Johnson emphasizes, "Do what you have to do to be successful...And Then Some!"

To contact the author for speaking engagements,

professional development sessions,

consulting or bulk sales, visit

DrDarrellJohnsonSpeaks.org

634 NE Main St, #1263
Simpsonville, SC 29681
HadassahsCrown@gmail.com
864-708-1214
"Publishing Excellence With Integrity"

Made in the USA
Lexington, KY
27 November 2019